CW00539431

MOYA CANNON was born in Dunfa
and now lives in Galway. She
University College, Dublin, and i
Christi College, Cambridge. She l
poems: *Oar* (Salmon Publishing,
Gallery Press, 2000) and *The Parc*
1997). She has been an editor of *Poetry Ireland Review* and writer-in-residence at Trent University, Ontario, and at the Centre Culturel Irlandais, Paris. In 1990 *Oar* was awarded the Brendan Behan Memorial Prize and in 2001 Moya Cannon was presented with the Lawrence O'Shaughnessy Award for Poetry. She was elected to Aosdána, the affiliation of Irish writers and visual artists, in 2004.

Irish poetry from Carcanet Press

EAVAN BOLAND
Selected Poems
New Collected Poems
Domestic Violence

JOHN F. DEANE
Toccata and Fugue: New and Selected Poems
Manhandling the Deity
The Instruments of Art

GREG DELANTY
The Blind Stitch
The Ship of Birth
Collected Poems 1986-2006

PADRAIC FALLON
'A Look in the Mirror' and other poems
'The Vision of MacConglinne' and other plays

THOMAS KINSELLA
Collected Poems

PETER MCDONALD
Pastorals
The House of Clay

PAULA MEEHAN
Dharmakaya

SINÉAD MORRISSEY
There Was Fire in Vancouver
Between Here and There
The State of the Prisons

MARY O'MALLEY
The Boning Hall
A Perfect V

JOHN REDMOND
Thumb's Width

PAULA MEEHAN, MARY O'MALLEY, EAVAN BOLAND
Three Irish Poets: An Anthology edited by Eavan Boland

MOYA CANNON

Carrying the Songs

CARCANET

First published in Great Britain in 2007 by
Carcanet Press Limited
Alliance House
Cross Street
Manchester M2 7AQ

Poems from *Oar* were first published by Salmon Publishing in 1990 and in a
revised edition by The Gallery Press in 2000. Reprinted by permission of
The Gallery Press, Loughcrew, Oldcastle, County Meath, Ireland

Poems from *The Parchment Boat* were first published by The Gallery Press
in 1997. Reprinted by permission of The Gallery Press, Loughcrew, Oldcastle,
County Meath, Ireland

'Violin'(p. 94) was originally published in *The Parchment Boat* with the title 'Viol'.

A CIP catalogue record for this book is available from the British Library

ISBN 978 1 85754 922 5

The publisher acknowledges financial assistance from Arts Council England

Typeset by XL Publishing Services, Tiverton
Printed and bound in England by SRP Ltd, Exeter

For John Moriarty

Acknowledgements

Some of the more recent poems in this volume have appeared in the following publications: *Winter Birds* (limited edition art book; Traffic Street Press, in association with the University of St Thomas, St Paul, Minnesota 2005); Walter Pfeiffer, *Connemara and Beyond*, (photographs of Connemara, with poems by Nuala Ní Dhomhnaill and Moya Cannon; Walter Pfeiffer Press, Wicklow 2005); Seamus Cashman (ed.), *Something Beginning with P: New Irish Poetry for Young Readers* (O'Brien Press, Dublin 2004).

Acknowledgements are also due to the editors of the following journals and magazines where some of these poems appeared for the first time: *Agenda, The Canadian Journal of Irish Studies, The Clifden Anthology, Crannóg, Five Points, Irish Pages, The Irish Times, The New Hibernia Review, The Oxford Magazine, Parabola, Poetry Ireland Review, The Review of Women's Studies* (National University of Ireland, Galway), *Ropes, The Shop.*

I wish also to thank Aosdána; the Arts Council of Ireland; the Centre Culturel Irlandais (Paris); Waterford City Council; the Verbal Arts Centre, Derry; the University of St Thomas, St Paul, Minnesota; and the Virginia Centre for the Creative Arts for their support during the writing of these poems.

I am very grateful to Kathleen Furey for permission to use her painting for the cover illustration and to The Gallery Press for granting permission to reprint poems from *Oar* and *The Parchment Boat.*

Contents

I

II

from *Oar*

from *The Parchment Boat*

I

Winter Birds

I have frequently seen, with my own eyes, more than a thousand of these small birds hanging down on the sea-shore from one piece of timber, enclosed in their shells and already formed.

Giraldus Cambrensis, *Topographia Hiberniae*

From the cliffs of Northern Greenland
the black-breasted geese come down
to graze on the wind-bitten sedges of Inis Cé.
They land in October, exhausted,
bringing with them their almost-grown young.

No one on these shores could ever find their nests,
so in early times it was concluded
that they had hatched from the pupa-shaped goose barnacle –
as fish, they were eaten on Fridays.

In April they gather now, restless, broody,
fatted on the scant grasses of a continent's margin,
ready to leave for breeding grounds in Greenland's tundra.

Watching that nervous strut and clamour –
a tuning orchestra raucous before the signal
to rise on the wind
in a harmony
old as hunger –
the name grips somewhere else,
my father's talk of 'winter-birds' in his class
in South Donegal,
the name his schoolmaster had given
to big boys and girls
who sat in the back seats,
back from the Lagan,
bound soon for Scotland,
already seasoned,
their migratory patterns set.

Carrying the Songs

for Tríona and Mairéad Ní Dhomhnaill

Those in power write the history, those who suffer write the songs
Frank Harte

It was always those with little else to carry
who carried the songs
to Babylon,
to the Mississippi –
some of these last possessed less than nothing
did not own their own bodies
yet, three centuries later,
deep rhythms from Africa,
stowed in their hearts, their bones,
carry the world's songs.

For those who left my county,
girls from Downings and the Rosses
who followed herring boats north to Shetland
gutting the sea's silver as they went
or boys from Ranafast who took the Derry boat,
who slept over a rope in a bothy,
songs were their souls' currency
the pure metal of their hearts,

to be exchanged for other gold,
other songs which rang out true and bright
when flung down
upon the deal boards of their days.

Timbre

A word does not head out alone.
It is carried about the way something essential,
a blade, say, or a bowl,
is brought from here to there when there is work to be done.
Sometimes, after a long journey,
it is pressed into a different service.

A tree keeps its record
of the temper of years
well hidden.

After the timber has been sawn
rough rings release the song of the place –
droughts, good summers, long frosts –
the way pain and joy unlock in a voice.

Our Words

Our words are cart-ruts
back into our guttural histories;
they are rabbit-tracks, printed
into the morning snow on a headland;
they are otter runs,
urgent between fresh and salt water;
they are dunlin tracks at the tide's edge.
They will be erased by the next wave
but, in the meantime, they assure us
that we are not alone
and that we are heirs to all the treasure
which words have ever netted.

Abetted by trade winds, they cross channels, oceans.
Seeds in the mud of a soldier's boot, they come ashore,
part, at first, of an arrogant, hobnailed scrape,
language of the rough-tongued *geurrier*.

But time does forgive them,
almost forgives them conquest –
Hard slangs of the market-place
are ground down to pillow-talk
and, as the language of conquest
grows cold in statute books,
elsewhere, its words are subsumed
into the grammars of the conquered

I be, you be, he bees.

The new words are golden, glamorous.
Grown old, they are dark pennies,
old friends to oxtercog us home.

And although so many
will be wiped out by the next wave,
we will never run short
because a mill on the ocean floor grinds them out,
keeping the tongue salt.

First Poetry

for Henry and Deirdre Comerford

These were, perhaps, the original poetry
swallows, terns, or grey-lag geese,
returning, unnoticed at first,
over the sea's rim,
or through the same dip in the hills,
in tune with the lift and fall of the seasons,
returning from nowhere,
or from an unknown terrain
which must consequently exist –

> *the warm countries,*
> *the frozen regions,*
> *the isles of the blest,*
> *Indies of the mind.*

They needed, for no obvious reason, two worlds
in which to feed and breed,
so they needed a capacity for sustained flight,
a fine orientation,
an ability to sleep on the wing
an instinct for form and its rhythms
as each took its turn to cut the wind.

As they flocked or spelled their way high over April
they needed hunger, and faith
and vital grace.

Forgetting Tulips

for Brídín and Kathleen

Today, on the terrace, he points with his walking-stick and asks
'What do you call those flowers?'

On holiday in Dublin in the sixties
he bought the original five bulbs for one pound.
He planted and manured them for thirty-five years.
He lifted them, divided them,
stored them on chicken wire in the shed,
ready for planting in a straight row,
high red and yellow cups –

treasure transported in galleons
from Turkey to Amsterdam, three centuries earlier.
In April they sway now, in a Donegal wind,
above the slim leaves of sleeping carnations.

A man who dug straight drills and picked blackcurrants,
who taught rows of children parts of speech,
tenses and declensions
under a cracked canvas map of the world –
who loved to teach the story
of Marco Polo and his uncles arriving home,
bedraggled after ten years' journeying,
then slashing the linings of their coats
to spill out rubies from Cathay –

today, shedding the nouns first,
he stands by his flowerbed and asks,
'What do you call those flowers?'

Augers

There were rusted augers scattered about the house,
ancestors of the brace-barrel and the electric drill,
owned by the old electrician who had lived here before me.
He was the youngest apprentice, perhaps, in a scratched photo
of the Galway Electrical Company, 1910 – the boy in a baggy, flat cap,
seated, cross-legged, in front of older working-men,
all grimly yet gamely posed,
a crew embarking to illuminate dark streets.
I kept the largest auger as a poker for the range,
kept it for luck,
investing it with a sense of augury.

Last summer I heard of a second set of augers.
When my Erskine grand-uncles, the last three
left Kilcar for Chicago,
their four siblings gone before them,
they pulled the door closed behind them,
not bothering to lock it.

Their valuables had been left with neighbours
who, three-quarters of a century later,
returned them to my cousin –
a bundle of augers for fixing boats.

Seven Edward Erskines had fished off the same white strand
since the first one had come from Scotland
and had married in.

He had hardly brought the augers with him,
but the word was already well travelled,
essential gear, tucked away in the holds of many boats,
having navigated northern coasts, centuries,
having tested the grain of languages, dialects –
Nafarr, nafogār, nave-gār, auger, boat-spear.

Demolition

On the gable of the adjoining house
at first-floor level, high above the people running to work
a rectangular black smudge shows where the range used to be.
To the left of the smudge,
there is a recess with six shelves.
On the fourth shelf up is half a bag of self-raising flour
with the top folded down.
Below it are a tin of Royal Baking Powder
and a glass salt cellar.

And something about this hurts badly
but I don't know what
or why I now remember waking at four in the morning,
long ago, the day after a love ended abruptly,
feeling that the room had no walls,
and that the winds of the world blew across my bed
and that I had no shelter
or hope of shelter.

It's strange that in this exposed, vanished house,
it's not the bedroom walls with their ripped, primrose wallpaper
and their little fireplaces which bother me,
but the sliced-off kitchen,
the abandonment
of leaven and savour.

Oughterard Lemons

In Paup Joyce's garden in the nineteen-sixties
in a council estate called The Lemon Fields,
it is said that there was a bush
with small lemons growing on it.

An O Flaherty of Aughanure Castle
had once shipped the trees from Spain
and had planted his land with them.

Stranger things had rooted
had almost gone native –
tubers from the Americas some voyager had brought back –
so why not this counterpoint to honey,
like honey, a love-child of the sun.

A whiff of spice roads
and we drag dreams home from our journeys –
necessary evidence of other climates,
other ways of growing –

and some dreams do take root in the quotidian,
as surely as fuchsia rampages along a side-road,
and some dreams sustain us totally, then fail us totally

and some hardly take at all
but survive in the tang of a placename,
in a crazy bush tilted by the wind.

Golden Lane

After a Christmas of rain and gales
there are four bright days
one after the other
at the start of January.

Across the lit milk of the bay
the sun hammers a path from Black Head to the prom,
a golden lane fit for any god
of winter, or light,
or life
and strong enough for three teenagers in red jackets,
their arms held wide,
to play at walking out over the tide,
into the sun's heart.

Today it feels likely
that this is where early stonemasons,
who built tombs
with shafts to channel midwinter light,
marked the day that the sun stopped falling,
discovered that light at its lowest is most intense.

This early, winter's evening it feels likely
that the sun's habits were first charted,
not on land,
but on a bright arm of the sea
which illumined the path
of a low sun returning.

Indigo

The indigo ridge
behind Benlettery horseshoe –

in late October light
it cut the early evening sky
and then the mountains fell down, down,
into deep Lough Inagh
and my heart
travelled the whole height and depth of them.

Rún

An trí rud is sciobtha san fharraige, an rón, an roc agus an ronnach.
(The three fastest things in the sea, the seal, the ray and the mackerel.)
Gaelic, traditional

Sudden as a cormorant
the black head broke
through the silk of the morning estuary,
turned,
and swam near enough to the pier
for me to see two soft dents.

It watched for a long time,
curious
and silent,
against the grind of building sites,
the clatter and scrape of the docks,
the uneven hum of cars.

Then it tossed its nose in the air
and sank, on its back, down into its own world.

Before that I hadn't known that they were here.
Afterwards I'd stop and watch the channel for them.
A shimmer of rattled foil
showed that one was coming up
or had just gone.

Sometimes one would whack the water with its hind flippers
and leap up
leaving a brightness in my day,
so that I felt grateful
that it had stopped fishing
long enough to observe our frenzy
and somehow, to calm it.
Then, one day, further west,
I saw a colony of them,
warm slugs clustered on the seaward side of a rock –
one of the three fastest creatures in the sea,
one of the slowest and most awkward on land.

Their sea-black pelts
had turned golden in the sun
and I realised
how much they need this element too.
This is where they breed.
This is where they breathe.

Rún: Gaelic, secret.

Starlings

Some things can't be caught in words,
starlings over an October river, for instance –
the way they lift from a roof-ridge in a cloud
directed by a hidden choreographer;
the way they rise, bank and fall,
tugging at some uncharted artery of the human heart;
the way the cloud tilts, breaks and melds,
the undersides of wings garnering all the light
that's left in an evening sky;
the way they flow down onto a warehouse roof,
bird by brown bird.

Bright City

I follow the morning light down the canal path,
across the road and on to the Claddagh.
In light which has turned canal, river and estuary to mercury,
even the cars on the Long Walk are transfigured.

Five swans beat their way in past the mud dock,
heavy, sounding their own clarion,
carrying the world's beauty
in on their strong white backs this Saturday morning.

Stranger

After a week of walking
the angled streets and the hills
of the small city, with its towers and steel ships,
I wanted to be near a well.

And out past Dungarvan, I found one –
well-minded,
gravelled, full and quick.

The gale-driven rains of the past week
poured into the corner of it.
The hill was a pitcher
tilted forever
to fill
a worn stone cup.

Walking out to Island Eddy

for Carol Langstaff and Jim Rooney

At low spring tide in February, when the wind is right,
the moon hauls the sea back off the sand bar for an hour or two,
allowing us to walk out to an island of roofless houses.

We have stumbled down over wrack-draped stones
and have waited, as, yard by yard,
a warm arm of sand rises out of the tide.

We wade the first few yards,
water lapping to the tops of our wellingtons,
and come up onto a road
of coarse, gold-and-indigo sand
and purple scallop fans.
Sarah says, 'This is how the Israelites crossed the Red Sea.
They must have known the tides.'

Behind us, a man, his grown son
and a dog have been driving
a flock of black-faced sheep along the grassline.
Now, they head them down,
through pools, bladderwrack and kelp.

One sheep is handled through the last of the ebbing tide.
The others scatter, bleating,
but are gathered up and herded
onto their sea-path, their path to summer grass.

We stand aside to let them pass.

Their hooves crush and crush loudly into the seabed
as they trot between the upright flutes of razor shells
and the tiny, breath-driven geysers of the clams.

Sheep at Night in the Inagh Valley

for Leo and Clare

Maybe the dry margins draw them,
or grass, sprouting among limestone chippings –
they are here, as always,
on the edge of the tarmac
on a bend.

They shelter under clumped rushes –
white bundles in the night –
their eyes are low green stars,
caught in the trawl of my car's headlights.

Occasionally one hirples across the road
but, usually, they stay put
and gaze at the slowed-down car.

I envy them their crazy trust.

Weaning

He carried a lamb
up over the bog to the hill,
took sugar from his pocket and let it lick.

The clean tongue searched the crevices of his hand,
then he set it down to graze.

It would never stray from that hill,
tethered by a dream of sweet grass.

Whin

Before we'd heard of Van Gogh
we'd felt the hit of that yellow
when all the worst fields were rough-brushed,
overrun with a coconut-scented bush.

Barbed saffron, it trumpeted summer.
To farmers, it was a bright curse,
its rootball so tough and springy,
my father, as a boy, had cut sliotars from it.

In May, it lit hills and headlands,
brash, it invaded the earth –
'I'd know you on a whin bush in Australia'
was said to someone unexpectedly met.

But how were we supposed to greet
in fifth or sixth class when we did, at last, meet
the English language's only synonym –
furze and gorse, those lonely, identical twins.

Sliotar: Gaelic, ball used in the game of hurling.

Barbari

Steering west through Barnes Gap, beyond Termon,
the granite hills fill the radio with hail,
obliterating Mozart
as they used obliterate the Sunday match.

West of here,
for the eighteenth-century traveller,
lay the Wilds of Donegal,
wild as Africa, but wetter.

From our side,
when I was a child,
an elderly neighbour told me,
of a story he had heard as a child,
of a father from Horn Head,
coming to the door
to counsel his sons
as they headed east for Scotland.

   — *Be yiz good boys now,*
   and once yiz go beyond Barnes Gap
   take every man for a rogue.

II

To Colmcille Returning

It's time now to dig down
through the shingle of Port a' Churaich,
to bring up the skeleton of ash and oak,
to stretch new skins over the ribs
and to turn the beak of your boat to the south-west.

For this time your journey must be,
not across the spine of Britain
but across the scarred back of Ulster,
across the Sperrins and into the Glens
down through the Mournes and Sliabh Gullion
and into the small rainy towns with their supermarkets,
their video stores and graveyards,
into all the farms with their sprayed barns and Land Rovers,
their certainties
and their hurt.

You'll make your landfall at Derry,
Maiden City of the Planter,
oak grove of Cenél Conaill
in the territory of Cenél nEóghain –
citadel or sanctuary,
it was always half-beleaguered
the Foyle water north, east and south of it,
and, to the west,
'a bogge most uncommonlie wette'.

And this time you may take off the blindfold
for your vision is needed
and we'll need every ounce of your diplomacy,
you, who, in the middle of the path,
turned your back on much of what was native
and started out again
away from the carnage under Ben Bulben
and all your self-righteousness over the book,
you, who turned contrariness to grace
and scooped honey from the lion's skull.

Going for Milk

Coming on the *Stop* sign at night
on the bend of a side street,
I braked too fast,
too far from the barrier.

The soldier with the red torch
and the machine-gun
stepped back,
spoke to someone in the steel tower
then half-circled the southern car.

You'll be all right,
They won't do you a bit of harm if you don't scare them.

Every morning before school
I took the can,
crossed the road,
climbed into McGarvey's field,
stepped down sideways from the bottom step
to avoid the mud
and turned a corner behind Barlows'
to where cows lifted their horns out of the long grass,
started to move in.

Keep on going, they are far more afraid of you
than you are of them.

The soldier at the car window has a helmet too big for him,
is barely an adult, seventeen, eighteen maybe,
younger than my nephew, smaller.
He smiles, in relief.

Who sent him out?
Who sent any of them out,
telling them once more
absent-mindedly, maybe,
turning off the TV
or hanging a cup up on a hook,

They are all the same, that crowd,
trust none of them –
they're all tarred with the same brush.

And who is going to tell them the truth
which is not simple,
which sounds like the blackest lie
when they have stood in a kitchen
where killing was done –

They're not all the same.
Most of them are far more afraid of you
than you are of them.

Be careful now,
but go on over, the milk is needed.

Script

The double line of prints
showed where a pup had dragged itself up
a few yards above the tidemark.
It panted, blinking away the driven sand,
while a wind-ripped tide ebbed fast.

A few other November strays
arrived to taste the end of the gale –
a couple in blue raincoats, down for the weekend,
and two boys on bikes who'd heard the news.

Rested now, maybe, or scared,
it took off down the long white beach,
its blubbery weight gallumphing
as it pulled itself up and forward on its front flippers,
building up speed
until its flesh rippled and it was carried
as much by rhythm as by strength,
like the statues on Easter Island,
like ourselves.

It stopped, its sides heaving,
as if the small, grey-spotted body might burst
but gathered itself and set off
collapsing again, yards short of the water.

After a long time it raised its head,
hauled itself down the last slope of sand,
through the first thin broken waves, into its own depth
and then there was nothing
but the winter sea
and a double row of prints.

We walked down the shore for a closer look.
Dug hard into the sand,
claw-marks
recorded a breast-stroke,
a perfect, cursive script
which reached
the ocean's lip.

Shells

We used to hunker on the Silver Strand,
sifting the shells after a storm,
hunting for cowries.

The pink, furled nuggets were stored in jam jars,
hoarded in jacket pockets, on windowsills,
with pelicans' feet,
razor shells,
scallop shells,
turret shells
and the rare, white wentletrap.

Ignorant of how Venus had sailed ashore,
we were already intrigued
by all the felt asymmetries of the small sea-beasts' growth,
all the dizzy architecture
of the first flesh.

Survivors

This morning, at Catherine's Island,
the sea-potatoes are strewn along the tideline
like stranded souls.
Shorn of their soft, brown spines,
they are pieces of sea-porcelain.

Some are smaller than a fingernail,
others big as a baby's fist –
the sea's whitework,
translucent, nearly heart-shaped,
their innards freighted with sand.

I lift one to admire its pinpoint symmetries
and it falls apart –
I rinse another in the tide
and it falls apart –

but yesterday they rode out a North Atlantic gale
which churned the sea-bed, dug them up,
trundled them along in the roots of waves,
until their spines were worn off,
then swept them up here, on tufts of foam –

an impossibly safe landing
for frail coats of bone.

Breastbone

The loop of collar-bone is intact,
anchored still with sinew
to a perfect wind-keel;
the ribs are hollow straws;
the skewed shoulder-blades are thrown back
in the long curves of helmet-wings.

When I found it on the sand at Killehoey
it was already white,
clean of meat.

Light from the street
falls through its grained ivory
onto a page.

Nothing we make is as strong
or as light
as this.

Exuberance

i.m. Fergal O Connor

In the heatwave of seventy-six,
the year of our finals,
we tried to study opposite the library,
scorching ourselves by the square lake.
As students loped past
in frayed Levi's and cheesecloth shirts
we read Plato and Locke, Mill and Marx –
a palimpsest of world maps,
each one cancelling the last.
We drank coffee and talked
and fell awkwardly in and out of love.
Where, if anywhere, was truth?

The following summer, in County Louth
in the abandoned garden of Castle Roche
an exuberance of medieval herbs was found,
a physic garden, which had germinated
in the previous year's deep heat.
Possibly the herbs had come up often,
unrecorded by botanists,
unobserved among dandelions and docks.

Or possibly not – beside a sarcophagus,
in the Valley of the Kings
a bowl of wheat grains was found.
Three millennia after they had been entombed
to ensure nourishment in the next world,
some good grains were carried back
and they grew
in the moisture and the light of our time.

Banny

'As a child in Tyrone you'd be told
to banny the cat, to stroke it gently.
I suppose it comes from *beannaigh*,' she says.

She uses the word for the first time in eighty years, maybe,
as she rhythmically blesses her own old cat,
in its own tactile, enduring vernacular.

Beannaigh: Gaelic, to bless, to greet.

Orientation

A flock of seagulls
rocks on the water
at the sheltered end of Nimmo's pier –
the birds' white breasts all turned into the January wind.

Crystals in cooling magma
orient themselves to magnetic north
as towards a constant
although, over deep time,
poles shift about like bedrock or stars.

For us, who carry,
in our twined chromosomes,
all the wonder and terror
evolved within animal time and bone –

the carnage of our last century
and of the century just begun –
for us, might there be
some wandering pole or orient,

towards which some primal grain in us
might align itself, some kind of good,
some love, not absolutely constant,

but, within the time which comprehends us,
constant enough to draw us
like these seagulls, their tails and bills
the dipping points of compass needles.

Aubade

Every morning, this clear, February week,
at ten-to-seven, I've been drawn out of sleep
by this rich note –
far better than any rooster –
and such a strong song
from such a small,
black bird.

I wondered if the boiler had jolted him
out of his own dreams
and I re-timed it to see
but, bang-on ten-to-seven,
he was giving out the pay
from near the top of the apple tree,
lit up at another dawn
and quite oblivious that his song
was erasing my guilt
regarding last autumn's great crop
which had lain rotting,
pecked hollow, and rocking in the grass,
unbaked, unbottled,
or so I had thought.

Pollen

And this dust survives
through the deaths of ages.
It sleeps in deep layers of mud –
black, red and umber;
it sleeps under the wet pelt of a November hill
where long grass is the colour of fox;
it sleeps deep under lakes;
twelve metres down it survives,
dust of arctic meadows,
old and tough
as love.

Vogelherd Horse, 30,000 BC

Art, it would seem, is born like a foal that can walk straight away.
                                                                    John Berger

The horse is half the length
of my little finger –
cut from mammoth ivory
its legs have been snapped off,
three at the haunch,
the fourth above the knee
but its neck, arched as a Lippizaner's,
its flared nostrils,
are taut with life.

The artist or shaman who carved it
as totem, ornament or toy
could hardly have envisioned
that horses would grow tall
would be bridled, saddled,
that of all the herds of mammoths,
lords of the blond steppes,
not one animal would survive,
that the steppes would dwindle,
that, in the stacked mountains to the south,
rivers would alter course

but that this horse would gallop on
across ten thousand years of ice,
would see the deaths, the mutations of species
would observe the burgeoning of one species,
Homo faber, the maker,
who had made him,
or, who, using a stone or bone knife,
had sprung him from the mammoth's tusk,
had buffed him with sand,
taking time with the full cheeks, the fine chin,
and had set him down on the uneven floor
of the Hohle Fels cave
to ride time out.

Chauvet

for John Berger

One red line, defining his rump,
draws the small mammoth out of the cave wall,
renders him more than a stalagmite.

In another chamber,
a bear's paw protrudes,
outlined in charcoal.

The animals had been in the wall all along,
awaiting recognition, release.
The Stone Age artists knew it,

just as the Italian master would know it,
as his chisel unlocked perfect forms
from Carrara's marble,

as we know it,
when some informed, deft gesture –
a tilt in a melody,
a lit line in a poem or a song –
draws us out into our humanity,
warm-blooded, bewildered.

The Force

I used never notice this –
starlings rifling the ivy
for the last of last year's black fruit,
or green flames erupting
from the bronze bark of the apple tree.

I used to see primroses, all right –
warm banks of them
and fields of daffodils
in front of old peoples' houses,
and house-martins moulding mud nests
under the eaves –

but I never noticed the tall leaves of iris or montbretia
rise from the brown swirl of last year's withering,
or heard the roundness in the blackbird's throat –
I had no notion of that dogged, sullen power
which shoves up,
year after battered year,
as the earth's hot kernel
picks up its flagging conversation with the sun,

in a language of wingbeat
and pungent earth
and silk parting bark.

Lamped

I had left Streedagh Strand behind me,
with the Atlantic white and rough in the October dusk
when it started to rise,
left of the Ox mountains.
First, it was a lit blip and then,
a silver lid lifting out of cloud.

As the hunters' moon shed
its last rigid wisp of cloud,
I steered north and it rode high to my right –
a lamp to guide or stun
night animals, insects, birds.

All the way north it held high
until, at Barnesmore Gap
it lifted over the right-hand hill
and struck Lough Mourne across the middle,
struck it silver in the black bog.

I drew in on the grass
because this was the same as a moon lake
which I'd seen from a mountain top
as I was leaving childhood.

And here I was, once again,
lamped.

from
Oar

Eagles' Rock

Predators and carrion crows still nest here,
falcons, and this pair of ravens
that I first heard when I reached the cairn
and noticed a narrow skull among the stones.

Here, further east at the cliff,
their wing-tips touch the rock below me,
and leave,
and touch again.

Black as silk, they know their strong corner of the sky.
They circle once
and once
and once
and once again and soar out
to sweep their territory of bright grey hills.

There are green slashes down there,
full of wells and cattle,
and higher places, where limestone, fertile,
catacombed, breaks into streams and gentians.

Predators have nested here in late winter,
have swung against this face –
feather arrogant against stone –
long enough to name it.

Once Colman, the dove saint,
lived under this cliff,
left us his oratory, his well,
and his servant's grave.

The eagles are hunted, dead,
but down among the scrub and under the hazels
this summer's prey tumbles already
out of perfect eggs.

Holy Well

Water returns, hard and bright,
out of the faulted hills.

Rain that flowed
down through the limestone's pores
until dark streams hit bedrock
now finds a way back,
past the roots of the ash,
to a hillside pen
of stones and statues.

Images of old fertilities
testify to nothing more, perhaps,
than the necessary miracle
of water trapped and stored
in a valley where water is fugitive.

A chipped and tilted Mary
grows green among rags and sticks.
Her trade dwindles –
bad chests, rheumatic pains,
the supplications, mostly, and the confidences of old age.

Yet sometimes,
swimming out in waters
that were blessed in the hill's labyrinthine heart,
the eel flashes past.

Thirst in the Burren

No ground or floor
is as kind to the human step
as the rain-cut flags
of these white hills.

Porous as skin,
limestone resounds sea-deep, time-deep,
yet, in places, rainwater has worn it thin
as a fish's fin.

From funnels and clefts
ferns arch their soft heads.

A headland full of water, dry as bone,
with only thirst as a diviner,
thirst of the inscrutable fern
and the human thirst
that beats upon a stone.

Oar

Walk inland and inland
with your oar,
until someone asks you
what it is.

Then build your house.

For only then will you need to tell and know
that the sea is immense and unfathomable,
that the oar that pulls
against the wave
and with the wave
is everything.

Thalassa

Having got up, decided to go home,
how often do we find ourselves
walking in the wrong direction.

Some echo under the stones
seduces our feet,
leads them down again
by the grey, agitated sea.

'Taom'

The unexpected tide,
the great wave,
uncontained, breasts the rock,
overwhelms the heart, in spring or winter.

Surfacing from a fading language,
the word comes when needed.
A dark sound surges and ebbs,
its accuracy steadying the heart.

Certain kernels of sound
reverberate like seasoned timber,
unmuted truths of a people's winters,
stirrings of a thousand different springs.

There are small unassailable words
that diminish Caesars;
territories of the voice
that intimate across death and generation
how a secret was imparted –
that first articulation,
when a vowel was caught
between a strong and a tender consonant,
when someone, in anguish
made a new and mortal sound
that lived until now,
a testimony
to waves succumbed to
and survived.

Taom: Gaelic: an overflowing, usually in the context of a great wave of emotion.

Tree Stump

Thrown up
on the stones
in a bad November,

tree stump
returned from an exile
amongst fish and cormorants.

For a week or a year
the ocean has salted your huge wound,
rocks have battered off your bark,
but the shipworms haven't riddled you.

Alive or dead,
there is little left of the slow strength
that filled a sky
when summer followed winter
and wind threw down the seeds.

I drag off bladderwrack
to look at the years
and find, hugged hard in the wilderness of your roots,
lumps of granite
that stunted
and informed your growth.

Turf Boats

Black hookers at anchor
shining sea cattle;
rough trees for masts
rooted in salt water;
built, not for slaughter,
but for a life-giving traffic.

Wide ribs of oak,
a human heart filled you
as you sailed out of Carna.
You came into Kilronan,
two sods went flying,
you carried fire to the islands,
lime to Connemara.

Hollow boats at the Claddagh,
hearts that beat in you
lie in granite-walled graveyards
from Leitirmullen to Barna,
finished with hardship,
the unloading of cargo,
the moody Atlantic
that entered the marrow,
and bright days off Ceann Boirne,
when wind struck the brown sails
and Ithaca was Carna.

Prodigal

Dark mutter tongue,
rescue me,
I am drawn into outrageous worlds
where there is no pain or innocence,
only the little quiet sorrows
and the elegant joys of power.

Someone,
businesslike in his desires,
has torn out the moon by its roots.
Oh, my tin king is down now, mother,
down and broken,
my clear-browed king
who seemed to know no hungers
has killed himself.
Old gutter mother,
I am bereft now,
my heart has learnt nothing
but the stab of its own hungers
and the murky truth of a half-obsolete language
that holds at least the resonance
of the throbbing, wandering earth.

Try to find me stones and mud now, mother,
give me somewhere to start,
green and struggling, a blade under snow,
for this place and age demand relentlessly
something I will never learn to give.

No Sense in Talking

What knot at the root of articulation is loosening,
have we said too much?
The old trees are coming down to the river to drink
and the young trees on the mountain
are tormented by this, their first autumn.
Who now can plant a finger on the loss
or deny the bereavement?

We thought only to bring clarity
out of the murk of utterance,
a modicum of control,
a necessary precision
and, perhaps, an elegance.

But we find
that in this damned garden by the river
we have bred pheasants;
it hardly matters whether we feed them or shoot.

Where now is the fine drive of abstraction,
where our dim talk on pillows?
Where are our black ships at anchor?
And, above all, of what use is it to us to know
that the old dirty languages still hold
touch in the ear,
lick in the ear,
secrets for everybody?

We are no longer everybody.
Half-individuated we suffer,
unable to assuage the hungers
in the head, the heart, the blood.
Our dreams differ now,
one from the other,
so that we cannot converse on pillows
and our gods quarrel endlessly.

We, who have conquered,
weep dry tears,
unable to lament our loss –
the tongue's tangle
of comfort and fear.

We know well that
if we had sense we would know
that the river is stealing the bank,
tugging it down streams by the long grass,
while under our feet,
leaves lie that are red as dragons
and the very stones are ambiguous.

Have we said too little
too clearly,
our parsimony a theft?
Who now is there to assert
that there was love among the barbarous daffodils
when leaves were green as spears?

Hills

My wild hills come stalking.
Did I perhaps after all, in spite of all,
try to cast them off,
my dark blue hills,
that were half the world's perimeter?
Have I stooped so low as to lyricise about heather,
adjusting my love
to fit elegantly
within the terms of disinterested discourse?

Who do I think I'm fooling?
I know these hills better than that.
I know them blue, like delicate shoulders.
I know the red grass that grows in high boglands
and the passionate brightnesses and darknesses
of high bog lakes.
And I know too how,
in the murk of winter,
these wet hills will come howling through my blood
like wolves.

The Foot of Muckish

People from our town on the coast
cut turf at the foot of Muckish.
Other than that,
it was beyond our pale.

But one evening, coming down off Muckish
when I was ten, a clumsy, dark-hearted child,
I came over the last shoulder
and the small black mountain opposite
rose up in a cliff
and rocked a lake between its ankles.

A sixpence,
a home for all the little dark streams,
a moon
in the miles of acid land.

Listening Clay

for Caitriona

There are sounds
that we can,
and do, trust;

    a gale in the trees,
    the soft click of stones, where the tide falls back,
    a baby crying in the night.

No one has ever mocked these sounds,
or tried to comprehend them.
They are too common to be bought or sold,
they were here before the word,
and have no significance in law.

Endlessly repeated,
immutable,
they are sounds without a history.
They comfort and disturb
the clay part of the heart.

Easter

We went down through gardens where the trees moved,
the gates to the swamp were thrown open
and we were lost to the sprouting earth.

We were down among the old easters
where passion unmade us into our elements.
In that warm dark, only the blind heart ploughed on
as though the terrain were known.

Scar

Why does it affect
and comfort me,
the little scar,
where, years ago, you cut your lip
shaving when half-drunk
and in a hurry
to play drums in public.

We step now
to rhythms we don't own or understand
and, with blind, dog-like diligence,
we hunt for scars
in tender places.

Eros

To be with you, my love,
is not at all like being in heaven
but like being in the earth.

Like hazelnuts
we sleep
and dream faint memories of a life
when we were high, green, among leaves;
a life given
in a time of callow innocence,
before storms came
and we all fell down,
rattled down cold streams,
caught in the stones,
while berries, seasons, flowed past.
Then quicker currents, elvers, dislodged us,
nudged us out into the flow,
rushed us down with black leaf-debris,
and swept on
forgetting us
on some river-bend or delta.

For us, drifted together,
this is the time when shells are ready
for that gentler breaking.

The deep and tender earth
assails us with dreams,
breaks us,
nourishes us,
as we tug apart
its own black crust.

Afterlove

for Colman

How could I have forgotten
the sickness,
the inescapability?
My strange love,
it frightens my life.
We sail high seas
and watch the voyages of stars.
Sometimes they collide.
Did you know, you make my head flame.
Blue flames and purple flames leap about my head.
I had once a thousand tongues
but tonight
my head is crashing through the sky,
my head is flaming on a dish.

My love,
carry it in carefully,
my love,
carry it in with trumpets.

Narrow Gatherings

At Portrush
the boarding houses are empty
even along the sea-front.
How quiet a Sunday
for after Easter.
Up to the tall houses
the pale tide flows
disturbed and beautiful,
the April sun barely brightens
its legendary cold.

Lir's children had it hardest here,
and here
the giants sculpted rock to honeycomb,
hammered back the great arched cliffs,
but failed to join two shores.

Encumbered by legend,
we are foreigners here
and know less
than we had imagined.

A band, practising in the town, winds
now out of wind-scraped streets,
the policeman first
and the great drums
that come and come like summer thunder

and then the flutes and fifes –
a music unexpected
as silver water collected
in the dark shoulders of hills, caught,
and gathered narrow for an instant
under high wrists,
until the wind splits it finely,
a young river scattering.

Under a low sun
the band is marching now
past the painted doors

and down along the promenade,
towards the cold shore and turning
until all the wind-snatched silver life strikes
bright against the tide:

And after
come the marching children,
growing smaller and smaller
in their uniforms.

Dark Spring

i.m. Feilimí Ó hUallacháin

Last night
the sky was still so full of light
the birds shouted in the empty trees
when, in the bone the dark cracked,
with so little sound,
almost no sound,
we did not hear it
but, incredulous, saw in our grief
the dark birds falling out of every tree
and after the birds the falling, dead, dark leaves.
Oh, we wept, we were not told,
we were not led to expect,
back when the thin bone knit to close the sky,
inside the skull-cave when we etched our myths
and later made our compacts with the ogre
we had no thought of this,
nor could we have schooled our hearts for this absurd
and sudden
sorrow.

Fair head
so vivid, in the loose wet earth.

In your death we are twice lost, twice bereaved,
all our compacts now dissolved,
we are so unexpectedly mortal.

Yet even
as we leave you
the sun flies down
to strike the dark hills green.
Defiant, it drives the pulse of summer
through this most desolate spring.

Wet Doves

Two wet doves are perched in the tree all afternoon.

On a day as rainy as this,
a bare apple tree is a poor place to roost.

Beyond my window
this tatty metaphor of love and fructitude huddles
and grubs under its oxters
and defecates and drips
and then
spreads two perfectly white fans
and flies away.

Nest

A brown wheel of reeds and broken willow
turns somnolently in a corner above the weir.
How long will that current hold it
before the flow sweeps it over?

Two Coke cans and a fast-food carton
are wound into the heart of it.

Out of habit,
god goes on making nests.

Crow's Nest

On St Stephen's day,
near the cliffs on Horn Head,
I came upon a house,
the roof-beams long since rotted into grass
and, outside, a little higher than the lintels,
a crow's nest in a dwarf tree.

A step up from the bog
into the crown of the ash,
the nest is a great tangled heart;
heather sinew, long blades of grass, wool and a feather,
wound and wrought
with all the energy and art
that's in a crow.

Did crows ever build so low before?
Were they deranged, the pair who nested here,
or the other pair who built the house behind the tree,
or is there no place too poor or wild
to support,
if not life,
then love, which is the hope of it,
for who knows whether the young birds lived?

After the Burial

They straightened the blankets,
piled her clothes onto the bed,
soaked them with petrol,
then emptied the gallon can
over the video and tape recorder,
stepped outside their trailer,
lit it, watched until only the burnt chassis was left,
gathered themselves
and pulled out of Galway.

Camped for a week in Shepherd's Bush,
then behind a glass building in Brixton,
he went into drunken mourning for his dead wife,
while their children hung around the vans,
or foraged in the long North London streets
among other children, some of whom also perhaps understood,
that beyond respectability's pale,
where reason and civility show their second face,
it's hard to lay ghosts.

Sympathetic Vibration

for Kathleen

'You never strike a note,
you always *take* the note.'

Did it take her many
of her eighty quiet passionate years
to earn that knowledge,
or was it given?

Music, the dark tender secret of it,
is locked into the wood of every tree.
Yearly it betrays its presence
in minute fistfuls of uncrumpling green.

No stroke or blade can release the music
which is salve to ease the world's wounds,
which tells and, modulating, retells
the story of our own groping roots,
of the deep sky from which they retreat
and, in retreating, reach –
the tree's great symphony of leaf.

No stroke or blade can bring us that release
but sometimes, where wildness has not been stilled,
hands, informed by years of patient love,
can come to know the hidden rhythms of the wood,
can touch bow to gut
and take the note,
as the heart yields and yields
and sings.

Foundations

Digging foundations for a kitchen,
a foot and a half below the old concrete
they open a midden of seashells.

This was once called 'kitchen' –
poor man's meat, salty, secretive,
gathered at low spring tide.

Blue mussels creaked as a hand twisted them from the cluster,
limpets were banged off with a stone, lifted with a blade,
the clam's breathing deep in wet sand
gave a mark to the spade.

Backs ached, reaping the cold and succulent harvest.
How many were consumed?

A shovelful, two shovelfuls,
six barrowloads, are dug out and dumped –
the midden runs under the wall
into the neighbour's yard.
The builder goes home, joking that he's found gold.

In a battered barrow, under the June evening sun,
the last shovelfuls turn palest gold.
They speak in silent sympathy
with all that has been exiled, killed and hidden,
then exhumed,
vulnerable again in the air of another age.

The taciturn clams break their silence to say,
'Dig us out if you need to,
position the steel,
raise the concrete walls,
but, when your shell is complete,
remember that your life,
no less than ours,
is measured by the tides of the sea
and is unspeakably fragile.'

Votive Lamp

The Pope and the Sacred Heart
went off on the back of a cart,
and I've tried to find a home
for the Child of Prague.

If that lamp weren't the exact
shape of a brandy glass, there might be some chance
that I'd part with it.

Small chance, though.
If I'd been brought up in the clear light
of reason,
I might feel differently.

But I often come home in the dark
and, from the hall door,
in the red glow
I can discern
a child's violin
and, coming closer,
a plover;
the photograph of a dead friend;
three hazelnuts gathered from a well;
and three leather-skinned shamans
who flew all the way from Asia
on one card.

I designed none of this and don't know whether
sacred objects and images tend to cluster
around a constant light,
or whether
the small star's constancy,
through other lives and other nights,
now confers some sanctity
on my life's bric-a-brac.

from
The Parchment Boat

Crannóg

Where an ash bush grows in the lake
a ring of stones has broken cover
in this summer's drought.
Not high enough to be an island,
it holds a disc of stiller water
in the riffled lake.

Trees have reclaimed the railway line behind us;
behind that, the road goes east –
as two lines parallel in space and time run away from us
this discovered circle draws us in.
In drowned towns
bells toll only for sailors and for the credulous
but this necklace of wet stones,
remnant of a wattle Atlantis,
catches us all by the throat.

We don't know what beads or blades
are held in the bog lake's wet amber
but much of us longs to live in water
and we recognise this surfacing
of old homes of love and hurt.

A troubled bit of us is kin
to people who drew a circle in water,
loaded boats with stone,
and raised a dry island and a fort
with a whole lake for a moat.

Shards

My garden is a graveyard for plates and cups
or else there's a bull in a china shop at the earth's core.
Each year's digging draws up a new hoard
and there's democracy in all the brokenness.
A blue pagoda lands next to a dandelion;
heavy delft and rosy wedding china
are beaten bright by the same May rain.
All equal now in the brown loam,
not all saw equal service or were mourned equally,
yet not one fragment gives anything away,
not a word of all they heard or saw,
or of the hands which used them roughly or with care –
dumb witnesses of hungers sated and thirsts slaked,
of the rare chances of communion,
before they were broken, and returned,
clay to clay,
having been through the fire
and having been a vessel for a while.

Introductions

for Brendan and Ursula

Some of what we love
we stumble upon –
a purse of gold thrown on the road,
a poem, a friend, a great song.

And more
discloses itself to us –
a well among green hazels,
a nut thicket –
when we are worn out searching
for something quite different.

And more
comes to us, carried
as carefully
as a bright cup of water,
as new bread.

Murdering the Language

Why did I love
the neat examination of a noun under the pointer,
the analysis of a sentence lifted out of talk,
canal water halted in a lock?

>*Mood, tense, gender.*
>*What performs the action, what suffers the action?*
>*What governs what?*
>*What qualifies, modifies?*

When we whispered in our desks
we spoke our book of invasions –
an unruly wash of Victorian pedantry,
Cromwellian English, Scots,
the jetsam and the beached bones of Irish –
a grammarian's nightmare.

But we parsed a small rectangular sea
and never missed the flow
or wondered why victories won in blood are fastened in grammar
and in grammar's dream of order;
or why the dream of order draws us as surely as the dream of freedom
or why correct language is spoken only in the capital.

Our language was tidal;
it lipped the shale cliffs,
a long and tedious campaign,
and ran up the beaches, over sand, seaweed, stones.

Laws learned by heart in school are the hardest to unlearn,
but too much has been suffered since
in the name of who governs whom.
It is time to step outside the cold schools,
to find a new, less brutal grammar
which can allow what we know:
that this northern shore was wrought
not in one day, by one bright wave,
but by tholing the rush and tug of many tides.

Hunter's Moon

There are perhaps no accidents,
no coincidences.
When we stumble against people, books, rare moments out of time,
these are illuminations –
like the hunter's moon that sails tonight in its high clouds,
casting light into our black harbour,
where four black turf boats
tug at their ropes,
hunger for the islands.

Ontario Drumlin

Having run out the boat,
what stop of the heart
causes us to beach on the half-known
as Colmcille dragged up his skin boat
on the white strand of Iona?
An exile surely,
but the same salt-shriven grass,
the same wind at his heels.

Or what in me longs enough for the diminutive
in a continent of trees,
for this name to grip
here beside the Otonabee?
Druimlín,
little back, little hill,
a glacier kernel
rounded and stony
as any in Ulster's Cavan,
though the trees on it are red
and the hill's real name
is not heard.

Patched Kayak

Royal Ontario Museum, Toronto

Who made the parchment boat?
Who bent and bound ribs of drifted wood
to a long clean frame?
Who stretched sealskins,
plaited sinew,
stitched the stitches?
Which mapped the making,
which mapped the wounds,
which curved along the edges of the lives of seals,
the edges of the lives of women,
the edges of the lives of men.

Oysters

There is no knowing,
or hardly any,
more wondering –
for no one knows what joy the stone holds
in its stone heart,
or whether the lark is full of sorrow
as it springs against the sky.
What do we know, for instance,
of the ruminations of the oyster
which lies on the estuary bed –
not the rare, tormented pearl-maker,
just the ordinary oyster?
Does it dream away its years?

Or is it hard,
this existence where salt and river water mix?
The endless filtering
to sustain a pale silky life,
the labouring to build a grey shell,
incorporating all that floods and tides push in its way,
stones, mud, the broken shells of other fish.

Perhaps the oyster does not dream or think or feel at all
but then how can we understand
the pull of that huge muscle beside the heart
which clamps the rough shell shut
before a hunting starfish or a blade
but which opens it
to let in the tide?

Tending

When a wood fire burns down and falls apart
the fire in each log dies quickly
unless burnt ends are tilted together –
a moment's touch, recognition;
gold and blue flame
wraps the singing wood.

Violin

Wherever music comes from
it must come through an instrument.
Perhaps that is why we love the instrument best
which is most like us –

a long neck,
a throat that loves touch,
gut,
a body that resonates,

and life, the bow of hair and wood
which works us through the necessary cacophonous hours,
which welds dark and light into one deep tone,
which plays us, reluctant, into music.

Viola d'Amore

Sometimes love does die,
but sometimes, a stream on porous rock,
it slips down into the inner dark of a hill,
joins with other hidden streams
to travel blind as the white fish that live in it.
It forsakes one underground streambed
for the cave that runs under it.
Unseen, it informs the hill,
and, like the hidden strings of the *viola d'amore*,
makes the hill reverberate,
so that people who wander there
wonder why the hill sings,
wonder why they find wells.

Arctic Tern

Love has to take us unawares
for none of us would pay love's price if we knew it.
For who will pay to be destroyed?
The destruction is so certain,
so evident.

Much harder to chart,
less evident,
is love's second life,
a tern's egg,
revealed and hidden
in a nest of stones
on a stony shore.

What seems a stone
is no stone.
This vulnerable pulse
which could be held in the palm of a hand
may survive
to voyage the world's warm and frozen oceans,
its tapered wings,
the beat of its small heart,
a span between arctic poles.

Milk

Could he have known
that any stranger's baby
crying out loud in a street
can start the flow?
A stain that spreads
on fustian
or denim.

This is kindness
which in all our human time
has refused to learn propriety,
which still knows nothing
but the depth of kinship,
the depth of thirst.

Winter Paths

There is something about winter
which pares all living things down to their essentials –
a bare tree,
a black hedge,
hold their own stark thrones in our hearts.

Once, after searching a valley,
summer after summer,
I went in winter
and found, at last, the path
that linked the well to the little roofless churches –
a crooked way through fields.
Leafless, fruitless, the briar-bound stone walls
revealed their irregular gaps –
the way cattle and goats
and women and men
had passed, winter after winter,
drawing aside or shoving past stray strands of briar,
wondering if they'd know their way again in summer.

Hazelnuts

I thought that I knew what they meant
when they said that wisdom is a hazelnut.
You have to search the scrub
for hazel thickets,
gather the ripened nuts,
crack the hard shells,
and only then taste the sweetness at wisdom's kernel.

But perhaps it is simpler.
Perhaps it is we who wait in thickets
for fate to find us
and break us between its teeth
before we can start to know anything.

Mountain

Beauty can ambush us, even through a car window.
This green galleon sails eternally through Sligo,
dragging our hearts in its wake.

One singer was found by hunters on these green flanks
and another chose them as a deep cradle for his bones
but neither the Fianna's chroniclers nor Yeats
did more than pay their respects
to what was already here –

a mountain
which had already
shaken off glaciers,
carried a human cargo,
known grace in stone.

It might have been the same February light
on these tender slopes
which drew the first people from the coast
to set their fires on this plateau,
to build on this great limestone boat
whose boards are made of fishbones,
whose water is green time.

Scríob

Start again from nothing and scrape
since scraping is now part of us;
the sheep's track, the plough's track
are marked into the page,
the pen's scrape cuts a path on the hill.

But today I brought back
three bones of a bird,
eaten before it was hatched
and spat or shat out with its own broken shell
to weather on the north cliffs of Hoy.

This is an edge
where the pen runs dumb.
The small bleached bones of a fulmar or gannet
have nothing to tell.
They have known neither hunger nor flight
and have no understanding of the darkness
which came down and killed.

Tracks run to an end,
sheep get lost in the wet heather.
There are things which can neither be written, nor spoken, nor read;
thin wing bones which cannot be mended.

Too fragile for scraping,
the bones hold in their emptiness
the genesis of the first blown note.

Thole-Pin

Who speaks of victory? Endurance is all.
                    Rainer Maria Rilke

Words, old tackle,
obsolete tools
moulder in outhouses, sheds of the mind –
the horse-collar rots on a high hook;
a flat-iron and an open razor rust together.

Sometimes a word is kept on
at just one task, its hardest,
in the corner of some trade or skill.
Thole survives,
a rough dowel
hammered into a boat's gunnel
to endure,
a pivot
seared between elements.

Easter Houses

During the last weeks of Lent
our play was earnest.
We'd hack sods out of the grass
and stack them among the trees
into four low walls.
The Easter house never had a roof –
what we needed was a place
where we could boil eggs outside.

After the battened-up heart of winter,
the long fast of spring,
life had come out again to nest in the open;
again, the shell was chipped open from within.

Song in Windsor, Ontario

Ice whispers
as it crushes against
steelbound, staggering timbers
in the Detroit river.

Great plates of ice from the lakes
catch on the banks,
turn under the March sun,
crumple each other
to show
how mountain ranges are made.

And on the wooden pylons,
a small bird
is back with the seed of music,
two notes,
the interval of desire
registered on the stirring cities.

Driving through Light in West Limerick

*Poetry,
surpassing music, must take the place
of empty heaven and its hymns.*
Wallace Stevens

What's light that falls on nothing?
Nothing.
But this light turns wet trees into green lamps
and roadside grass into a green blaze
and lets the saffron hills run through our hearts
as though the world had no borders
and wet whin bushes were deeper than the sun.

What's light,
and who can hold it?
This morning, across the sea, in a gallery
I saw light held for five hundred years
on an angel's face –
a moment's surprise,
and centuries fell away
quiet as leaves.

But the angel's features
had been no more than any perfect features
until they'd caught the light
or else the light had fallen on them.

And trying to figure out
which had happened
I got off the Underground at King's Cross
and an accordion tune filled
the deep steel stairwell.

This was some descent of the strong sun,
good music
brought down to where it was needed,
music surpassing poetry
gone down again,
the busker with a red *Paolo Soprani*

105

telling again
of Orpheus in Connacht.

The escalators ground up and down
carrying all the people
up and down a hill
of saffron light.

Attention

Sometimes there is nothing,
absolutely nothing,
to be done but watch
and wait
and let the clock which breaks our days
let go its grasp
until the mind is able
to trust the storm
to bear up our weight of flesh and bone
to take on the time of breath
the rhythm of blood
a rhythm held
between two breaths
a bright cry
a last rasp.

An Altered Gait

With the scurry of a sandpiper
a gull runs and runs along the tideline.
It trails something dark behind it,
the broken rim
of its right wing.

A fortnight ago
as my father lay dying
he sometimes lifted his good right arm,
the same troubled eye –
the same hurry told in his breath
as we waited
and he laboured
towards the flight out.

Bulbs

I put them down late, in November,
into the grass of the cold garden.
It is hard to believe that they will grow at all
or that the brown papery onions,
now stowed in the ground,
have life in them.

Yet before the frosts are finished
they will come up,
green spears through the grass,
like sleeping legions returning in our time of need.

That time is spring,
when courage is necessary and scarce,
when each green blade will break and yield up
last summer's hoarded sun.

Night

Coming back from Cloghane
in the sudden frost
of a November night,
I was ambushed
by the river of stars.

Disarmed by lit skies
I had utterly forgotten
this arc of darkness,
this black night
where the frost-hammered stars
were notes thrown from a chanter,
crans of light.

So I wasn't ready
for the dreadful glamour of Orion
as he struck out over Barr dTrí gCom
in his belt of stars.

At Gleann na nGealt
his bow of stars
was drawn against my heart.

What could I do?

Rather than drive into a pitch-black ditch
I got out twice,
leaned back against the car
and stared up at our windy, untidy loft
where old people had flung up old junk
they'd thought might come in handy,
ploughs, ladles, bears, lions, a clatter of heroes,
a few heroines, a path for the white cow, a swan
and, low down, almost within reach,
Venus, completely unfazed by the frost.

Migrations

The strong geese claim the sky again
and tell and tell and tell us
of the many shifts and weathers
of the long-boned earth.

Blind to their huge, water-carved charts,
our blood dull to the tug of poles,
we are tuned still to the rising and dying of light
and we still share their need
to nest and to journey.

Between the Jigs and the Reels

Between a jig and a reel
what is there?
Only one beat
escaped from a ribcage.

Tunes are migratory
and fly from heart to heart
intimating
that there's a pattern
to life's pulls and draws.

Because what matters to us most
can seldom be told in words
the heart's moods are better charted
in its own language –

the rhythm of Cooley's accordion
which could open the heart of a stone,
John Doherty's dark reels
and the tune that the sea taught him,
the high parts of the road and the underworlds
which only music and love can brave
to bring us back to our senses
and on beyond.